THE HEART OF
THE STORM

A BIOGRAPHY OF SUE BIRD

Sharon Mentyka   Illustrated by **Ellen Rooney**

little bigfoot

an imprint of sasquatch books
seattle, wa

Many years before that thrilling night, Suzy Bird was a feisty little girl who couldn't stop moving. As soon as she could walk—she ran, jumped, or climbed instead. This terrified her parents until they noticed how easily she moved, with quickness and grace. Then they worried less, and let her follow her heart.

That's our little bird!

Sue was naturally quiet and a little shy. In her sleepy little town on
Long Island, New York, she could play alone for hours, building a
private magical world all her own. But always, she grew restless.
Then it was time to go outside, where a whole world waited, ready
to be explored.

Sue was tougher than she looked, and bumps and bruises made her proud. Everything she loved and all her talents seemed to fit together like a beautiful puzzle. Suzy the Barbie doll player and Suzy the tree climber were simply different parts of the same person! And if someone didn't understand that—well, that was *their* problem.

Sue was perfectly comfortable being herself.

As Sue grew older, she discovered she had a remarkable memory. She could hear a song once and remember all the lyrics and recite whole movie scenes flawlessly. And she never worried about getting lost. She always knew how far she had gone, which turns she'd made, and how long it would take to make her way back home.

Sue adored her older sister, Jen. Wherever Jen went, Sue followed. Whatever new sport Jen tried, Sue wasn't far behind. Gymnastics, track, volleyball, swimming, tennis!

Soccer soon became a favorite. She paid close attention to how the game was played and practiced drills for hours. Before long, no local girls' teams were playing at her skill level. When an invitation arrived to join an all-boys team instead, she didn't hesitate.

It was a rocky start. Then the boys saw how well she could play, and all the teasing stopped.

One day, Jen picked up a basketball.

The rhythm, energy, and grace of the game quickly won Sue's heart. All you needed was a ball and a basket! She began spending as much time as she could shooting hoops in her driveway or playing one-on-one pickup games with her best friend, Brad. The two were evenly matched, and she learned to never give an inch.

Sue began to dream. Maybe one day, she would play in the Olympics!

Before long, the echo of bouncing basketballs in the gym seemed like the happiest sound in the world.

On the court, Sue was tall, but never the tallest. She was fast, but not the fastest. To compete at the highest level, she had to find other ways to win.

Her sharp memory and keen eye for spotting everything around her helped. The offense would start a play, and instantly Sue could imagine everyone's next move. People began to notice.

What helped the most? Sue hated to lose, and she did everything she could to make sure it didn't happen.

She was born in October, the tenth month, so she always chose ten as her uniform number. She tied her sneaker laces a particular way and always wore a straightened ponytail—with *two* hair bands, both the same color. Deep down, she knew these little routines wouldn't win games, but they helped her focus and feel prepared.

At sixteen, Sue's game was ready to blossom and she began yearning for a bigger challenge. It was an exciting time in women's basketball! A newly formed professional league—the Women's National Basketball Association (WNBA)—was about to play its first season.

A high school in nearby Queens, New York, had one of the strongest girls' basketball programs in the country. It was just twenty miles from her home but felt like a lifetime away from all she'd ever known and loved.

Basketball had given Sue so much joy, and she wanted more—so she decided to switch schools and follow her heart.

Christ the King High School opened up a whole new world for Sue. As the team's new point guard, she was challenged by her coaches to up her game, even when she felt uncomfortable. She already knew *how* to pass; now she needed to learn *when* to pass.

It helped to be surrounded by talented teammates. All the girls trusted each other, stuck together on the court and off, and tried to never make the same mistake twice. Playing for a top team like the Royals, Sue learned another important lesson—sometimes *thinking* you can win is just as important as actually winning.

There were not-so-happy times too, when her parents shared the news they would be separating. Sue knew it wasn't her fault, but her heart still felt heavy. She was grateful she could concentrate on her game instead.

After two state titles and an undefeated national championship, seven Royals seniors had their pick of college basketball scholarships, including MVP Sue! With its winning program, the University of Connecticut Huskies became her instant favorite. Plus, she'd be close to home!

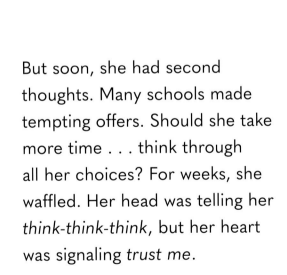

But soon, she had second thoughts. Many schools made tempting offers. Should she take more time . . . think through all her choices? For weeks, she waffled. Her head was telling her *think-think-think*, but her heart was signaling *trust me*.

Then the Huskies coach called.

"Well, I hope you follow your heart," was all he said.

That settled it.

With her talent for seeing every detail and thinking quickly on her feet, Sue earned the starting point guard position at UConn! It was a huge responsibility for a freshman, and expectations were high.

Sue inched her way onto the team, tense and cautious, making more turnovers than assists.

Then, one stormy December night, everything changed.

During an ordinary practice, on an ordinary jumper she'd made thousands of times before, she was running down the court, dribbling, eyeing her shot, when something in her left knee seemed to *pop*. Suddenly, her leg gave out and she crumbled to the floor. The pain was unbearable.

Her doctors delivered the bad news—the torn ligament in her knee would need surgery. She'd only played eight games for the Huskies!

Just like that, her first year of college basketball was over.

Now Sue faced a choice. She could feel sorry for herself, mope and moan about being on the sidelines . . . or she could look inside her heart. Maybe this was a chance to turn a bad experience into a positive one.

As a little girl, Sue had discovered the power of paying attention. Now she decided to use her time on the bench to study the beautiful game of basketball like never before. In the next six months, Sue learned more than she could ever have imagined, just by watching and listening.

The following season, with Sue back on the court, the Huskies came roaring back to win the NCAA championship!

But they didn't stop there.

Since their freshman year, Sue and her teammates had set their sights on playing in the WNBA after graduation. To prove they could do it, they took on a challenging goal—one that sometimes seemed unthinkable when the players were injured or exhausted. They wanted to go a *whole* season without losing even one game.

For the next two years, the women kept a laser focus. They practiced against the men's team to get better and stronger; they trusted their coach's vision, even when things seemed grim.

Private, shy Sue was now a vocal leader. She learned as much as she could about her teammates—their birthdays and favorite foods; when to push them to work harder, when to give them a hug—all with the goal of motivating them to win. Each had arrived at this special place in a different way. Now they were united, working toward a single goal.

It worked! The Huskies ended Sue's senior year setting a new school record—a perfect 39–0 season with Sue named College Player of the Year!

The end of the 2002 college season had arrived—time for the WNBA to select new players from the talent pool. When Sue's name was called as the number one overall draft pick by the Seattle Storm, her first thought was: all her hard work had paid off!

Her second thought—*Seattle . . . where was that exactly?*
Awfully far from New York, but that was okay. Sue was ready for a new adventure.

When Sue arrived in Seattle, it became clear from the opening tip-off that her rookie season as a professional basketball player would be very different from her college career. The league was full of powerful, strong-willed personalities—sometimes they clashed.

The Storm was also a young team, just three years old, and had finished the previous season in last place. Sue liked pressure; she thrived on it. What she wasn't used to was losing. She would need to pace herself, physically *and* emotionally, to make it through the season.

Determined and self-possessed, Sue rose to the challenge. To Sue, being on a team really meant teamwork. Sure, it felt great to drill a three-pointer into the net late in the game, but she was perfectly happy to be the playmaker to help her new team grow.

Besides, Suzy Bird *loved* basketball. Now she had a chance to do what she loved and get paid for it! Whenever she stepped onto the court, the whole world seemed to disappear. All that was left was the squeak of her sneakers, the sound of the ball pounding the wooden court, the *swish* as it passed through the net.

She felt like ten-year-old Suzy again, playing a pickup game with her old friend Brad in their neighborhood park on Long Island.

Sue hadn't really planned to stay in Seattle her whole career, but the years quickly passed. She ran games in a calm, confident way. Her teammates trusted her completely. With Sue as the heart of the Seattle Storm, the team became a force to be reckoned with in the WNBA.

Her success and reputation grew far and wide.

She accomplished her dream of going to the Olympics—five times!

During off-seasons, she delighted in playing overseas for Russia in an international league.

She circled the world, speaking and coaching at youth camps, clinics, and schools—thrilled to be the role model she once wished she'd had growing up.

And after twenty-plus years of playing ball, her sneaker collection outgrew her closet!

Wherever Sue traveled, Seattle—with its big-city vibe and small-town feel, and the *best* fans in the world— always beckoned her home. Soon, she couldn't imagine herself anywhere else.

Sue's contributions to the sport of basketball continue, but her legacy is a slam dunk after a career filled with so many accomplishments:

Two state titles, two NCAA Division I titles, four WNBA championships, five Olympic medals (all gold!), four World Cup gold medals, twelve WNBA All-Star appearances, 540-plus career starts, 3,000-plus assists, 6,490-plus points, countless awards, tons of hair spray, five broken noses, zillions of loyal fans who love her . . .

and one team, the Seattle Storm, in the city that won her heart.

A LEADER
ON AND OFF THE COURT

Sue Bird has called her performance in Game 5 of the 2018 WNBA Semifinals against the Phoenix Mercury (described on pages 2–3) as "the biggest, best moment of my career," and Seattle went on to sweep the Washington Mystics in the best-of-five finals. Yet remarkably, two years later, she helped lead the Storm to *another* championship—their fourth—just days before her fortieth birthday.

"Ultimately, competition isn't about defeating others," she has said, "it's about testing yourself." This says so much about Sue's motivation, her character, and her success. It's a big part of why people have been drawn to her throughout her long career. She puts great faith in the power of sports as a way for kids to learn quickly that you can't fake it. Work hard and you'll improve. Don't and you won't. It's that simple. Learning that truth early, on the playing field, is a great life lesson.

When Sue was growing up in the 1980s, watching professional female athletes compete on television wasn't as easily available as it is today. Sue recalls not having many female athletes she could look up to, so she embraces her position now as a role model— not only for women in collegiate basketball programs but also young girls who might be just starting out, shooting their first hoop! She wants all basketball fans and every kid who loves sports—girls *and* boys—to see women as strong, confident athletes.

Like many parents of sports-focused children, Sue's parents, Herschel and Nancy, sacrificed a lot to support her desire to focus so intently on basketball from an early age. Now Sue recognizes that it's her turn to

SUE PLAYING IN THE WNBA CONFERENCE SEMIFINALS AGAINST THE LOS ANGELES SPARKS, 2009

support others. Whether it's mentoring kids at sports camps and clinics, or speaking about the Seattle Storm's core values of equality, diversity, and inclusion, Sue's kindness and generosity show. She shares the importance of trusting your coach for on-the-court strategy, but knowing when to speak up if a situation makes you feel physically or emotionally uncomfortable.

In everything she does, Sue tries to demonstrate how to be strong while also being kind, and how to be self-possessed, which simply means you're comfortable in your own skin and don't need the outside world to tell you who you are. Sue welcomes attention but remains humble. She is aware that her popularity and success offer her a rare opportunity to use her voice to promote causes she believes in, including supporting the Black and LGBTQIA+ communities, encouraging people to vote, and working to achieve equal pay for women athletes. You can't fake the sincerity and openness that Sue Bird offers to her fans—it only develops from a secure self-image. Sue would say it grows out of being yourself, discovering what you love to do, and working day to day to become better at it. For some, maybe that love is sports. For others, it might be something else. What's most important is that once you discover your passion, grow and share that love with the world, just like Sue.

Thank you, Sue. You've given your adopted city countless hours of exciting basketball. Your love of Seattle has been abundantly matched by your fans. We can't wait to see what you'll be up to next!

TITLE IX AND WOMEN IN SPORTS

Women's basketball leagues in the United States date back to the 1930s, although most were short-lived or played exhibition games only. In 1978, the Women's Professional Basketball League was founded with eight teams, but lasted just three seasons.

In 1976, women's basketball made its debut at the Summer Olympics in Montreal, Canada (men's basketball had been an Olympic sport since 1936). For the next twenty years, until the founding of the Women's National Basketball Association (WNBA) in 1996, the Olympic Games were the only reliable showcase for the sport.

Title IX was the real game changer for opening up access and equal opportunity for women in sports. Title IX of the Education Amendments Act of 1972 prohibited discrimination on the basis of gender in educational institutions that receive federal funds. Any federally funded education program or activity, public or private—including sports for girls and women—from elementary schools to colleges and universities, were now required to offer equitable resources to women as well as men.

The changes were enormous. According to the Women's Sports Foundation, before Title IX, only one of twenty-seven girls participated in high school sports. By 2016 that number jumped to two of every five, with increases in nearly every sport, including basketball. Now we have athletes like Sue Bird—not *women* athletes; just athletes, period—for young girls (and boys) to look up to.

Yet despite their amazing accomplishments, Sue and other top players like Diana Taurasi, Brittney Griner, and Maya Moore still aren't very well-known. With a shorter WNBA season, many of the women head overseas to play in other countries, as Sue did for ten years, not just to keep up their game but also for the additional money. WNBA women's salaries are a fraction of the men's. With far fewer televised games and less marketing of the league itself, many of these accomplished women

athletes, Sue Bird included, are more recognized internationally than they are within the United States.

So the uphill climb for female athletes is still steep but worth it. There is nothing quite like watching women's sports to really understand how powerful girls and women can be, and the game of basketball is a uniquely beautiful expression of this power. Watching a well-executed play on the court is like seeing the unfolding of a choreographed dance.

The value of participation in sports is powerful—it helps young girls build not only fitness but also self-esteem, confidence, and spirit. As Sue would say, it helps you learn to be yourself!

SUE BIRD   #10

SEATTLE STORM

POSITION: GUARD

HEIGHT: 5' 9"   WEIGHT: 150 LBS

BORN: OCTOBER 16, 1980
IN SYOSSET, NEW YORK

COLLEGE: UNIVERSITY OF CONNECTICUT

ACCOMPLISHMENTS AND AWARDS

HIGH SCHOOL

- Two state titles with Christ the King High School (1997, 1998)

- Named state tournament MVP (1998)

- National high school championship (1998: 27–0)

COLLEGE

- Two-time NCAA champion at UConn (2000: 36–1; 2002: 39–0) with an overall win-loss record of 114–4 in games played

- Two-time All-American

- Recipient of Wade Trophy and Naismith College Player of the Year (2002)

- UConn's all-time leader in three-point field goal (.459) and free throw (.892) percentage

WNBA

- Number one overall draft pick in round one by the Seattle Storm (2002)

- Twenty seasons with the Seattle Storm

- Four-time WNBA champion (2004, 2010, 2018, 2020)

- Twelve WNBA All-Star appearances (league record)

- All-time WNBA assist leader (3,000) and first in WNBA history to reach the 3,000 mark

- All-time WNBA leader in career starts (540); has never come off the bench in her career

USA BASKETBALL

- Record five-time Olympic gold medalist (2004, 2008, 2012, 2016, 2020)

- Four-time FIBA World Cup gold medalist (2002, 2010, 2014, 2018)

- One of only eleven players to have earned an NCAA title, a WNBA title, and an Olympic gold medal (Swin Cash, Tamika Catchings, Cynthia Cooper-Dyke, Asjha Jones, Maya Moore, Ruth Riley, Breanna Stewart, Sheryl Swoopes, Diana Taurasi, and Kara Wolters)

OVERSEAS

- Five-time Euroleague champion (2007–2010, 2013)

- Five-time Russian National League champion (2007, 2008, 2012–2014)

TIMELINE

Sue Bird's life and career have grown along with professional basketball opportunities for women. In this timeline, key events in the development of the history of basketball are noted with blue dots and dates. Milestones and personal accomplishments in Sue's life are highlighted in green. Overlapping dates contain both colored dots.

1891

James Naismith, a Canadian American physical education teacher and sports coach, develops a game using two peach baskets and a soccer ball to be played indoors during the cold winters in Springfield, Massachusetts, and calls it "basket ball."

1892

Senda Berenson, a physical education director at Smith College for women in Boston, Massachusetts, meets James Naismith and teaches a version of his game to her students, hoping to improve their physical health.

1893

Berenson organizes the first women's basketball game of Smith College sophomores against freshmen, with modified rules. No male spectators are allowed. Within two years, there are hundreds of women's collegiate basketball teams.

1949

The National Basketball Association (NBA) is formed.

1972

The US Congress passes the Education Amendments Act. Title IX of the law prohibits discrimination against girls and women in federally funded education, including in athletic programs.

1976

Women's basketball debuts at the Summer Olympics in Montreal, Quebec, Canada.

1991

Sue joins the Amateur Athletic Union (AAU) basketball league in Syosset, playing for the Liberty Belles, coached by Jill Cook and Vincent Cannizzaro.

1996

Sue transfers for her junior year to a private Catholic school in Queens, New York, to play with the Royals, coached by Cook, Cannizzaro, and Bob Mackey.

The Women's National Basketball Association (WNBA) is founded after the US women's team wins gold at the Summer Olympics in Atlanta, Georgia.

1997

Sue commits to the University of Connecticut under coach Geno Auriemma, after being recruited by many schools, including Vanderbilt and Stanford. Six other Royals earn college basketball scholarships.

2006

Sue acquires Israeli citizenship, through her father's Ukrainian-Jewish heritage (the original family name is Boorda).

2013

Sue sits out the entire season after knee surgery.

2015

Sue scores her 5,000th career point on August 2 in a game against the New York Liberty, becoming the first player in WNBA history to record 5,000 career points and 2,000 assists.

The Women's Minor League Basketball Association (WMLBA) is founded to give women additional opportunities as professional athletes.

2017

Sue comes out as gay in a joint appearance with her girlfriend, soccer star Megan Rapinoe.

1901

Berenson publishes *Basket Ball for Women*, outlining her women's rules for play.

1906

The Intercollegiate Athletic Association is formed to regulate national college athletic standards; it adopts its present name, the National Collegiate Athletic Association (NCAA), in 1910.

1936

The All-American Red Heads, a women's league whose members dyed their hair red, begin touring the country playing exhibition games against men.

1978

The Women's Professional Basketball League, comprised of eight teams, begins playing and lasts for three seasons.

1980

Suzanne Brigit Bird is born on October 16, 1980 in Syosset, Long Island, New York.

1986

Sue joins the Catholic Youth Organization (CYO) basketball league.

Margaret Wade, who coached Delta State to three national championships in the 1970s, becomes the first woman and first women's coach to be inducted into the National Basketball Hall of Fame in Springfield, Massachusetts.

1998

Sue enrolls in the University of Connecticut as part of the top recruiting class in the country that includes Swin Cash, Asjha Jones, and Tamika Williams, but is injured and sits out her freshman year after only eight games.

2002

Sue is selected as the number one overall pick in the WNBA draft by the Seattle Storm; her teammates Cash, Jones, and Williams are also selected in round one, the first time one school received four of the top six picks.

2004

Sue begins competing for Russia in the off-season; continues to play through 2014 with the Dynamo Moscow, Spartak Moscow, and UMMC Ekaterinburg.

2018

Sue breaks her nose for the fifth time; appears with Rapinoe as the first openly gay couple on the cover of *ESPN The Magazine*'s "The Body Issue."

2020

After missing the entire 2019 season due to knee surgery, Sue leads the Seattle Storm to their fourth WNBA championship ten days before her fortieth birthday; announces her engagement to Megan Rapinoe.

2021

Sue teams up with soccer star Alex Morgan, snowboarder Chloe Kim, and swimmer Simone Manuel to create TOGETHXR, a media company focused on narrowing the gender inequality gap in media coverage of women in sports.

GLOSSARY

Assist: when a player passes a ball to a teammate in a way that leads to scoring a field goal

Defense: the team currently without possession of the ball, who try to steal the ball, block or deflect passes, or gain possession through turnovers or rebounds

Division I (DI): the highest level of college athletic competition authorized by the National Collegiate Athletic Association (NCAA) in the United States

Draft: an annual event dating back to 1947 where teams from the professional leagues, such as the WNBA, can select eligible players, usually college athletes

Draft pick: selected players who are obligated to play for the teams that select them, unless they withdraw from consideration that year. The WNBA holds three rounds in their annual draft, each with thirty picks.

Dribbling: advancing the ball by bouncing it on the floor with one hand while walking or running down the court yourself, as opposed to passing it to another player or shooting for the basket

Field goal: a score made by any attempt other than a free throw; worth either two or three points, depending on the distance of the shot from the basket

Foul: a penalty usually called because of illegal personal contact with a player from the opposing team

Free throw: an unopposed attempt to score one point by shooting from behind a line at the end of a restricted area on the court after a foul on the shooter by the opposing team

Layup: a one-handed shot made from near the basket, often after a rebound, that ends in a score

Ligament: a short band of tough but flexible connective tissue that connects two bones or holds together a joint

Motivation: the reasons that guide a person to accomplish a goal

MVP: most valuable player

NCAA: the National Collegiate Athletic Association, the organization that regulates sports games for college athletes in North America

Offense: when the ball is moved down the court toward the basket by passing from one player to another or by dribbling

Off-season: the time of year when a particular sport is not played. In the WNBA, the regular season is played from May to September.

Olympics: a major international sporting event featuring summer and winter sports, where thousands of athletes from around the world participate in a variety of competitions

Pickup game: a game started by one or more players without planning

Pivot: when the player holding the ball keeps one foot in place on the ground while moving or turning with the other

Point guard: one of five positions in regulation basketball, which includes two guards, two forwards, and a center. Point guards are often called the "coach on the floor" because they run the team's offense by controlling the game and

making sure the ball gets to the right player at the right time.

Professional or **pro:** someone working in a specific field or activity for pay rather than as a hobby

Rebound: when a player gains control of the ball after a missed field goal or free throw

Recruiting: the process of adding prospective student-athletes to college teams through the offer of an athletic scholarship to a high school junior or senior

Rookie: a player's first year of playing their sport professionally, usually for pay

Self-possessed: confident; secure and sincere with yourself and others

Shot clock: a clock that controls the amount of time the team on offense is given to shoot the ball

Sidelines: the long, inactive areas on a basketball court. A term often used when a player is injured or removed from a game and cannot play.

Starter: the five players who start the beginning of a game, usually the best at their positions

Three-pointer: a field goal made from beyond the three-point line (approximately twenty-two feet in WNBA play), which is an arc marked on the court that surrounds the basket

Tip-off: the start of the game, or any extra period, where two opposing players try to gain control of the ball after an official tosses it into the air between them

Turnover: when a team loses possession of the ball to the opposing team

WNBA: the Women's National Basketball Association, a professional basketball league in the United States currently composed of twelve teams

For every child, may you find the bravery and wisdom
to be yourself. And for Mark, thanks for the "assists." —SM

For Sandra: friend, mentor, and the best
art-and-design floor general in the business. —ER

Manufactured in China by C&C Offset Printing Co. Ltd. Shenzhen, Guangdong Province, in October 2021

LITTLE BIGFOOT with colophon is a registered trademark of Penguin Random House LLC

26 25 24 23 22   9 8 7 6 5 4 3 2 1

Editor: Christy Cox
Production editor: Bridget Sweet
Designer: Alicia Terry

Photo of Sue Bird (page 40): © Brandon Parry/Southcreek Global/ZUMAPRESS.com
ZUMA Press, Inc. / Alamy Stock Photo

Library of Congress Cataloging-in-Publication Data
Names: Mentyka, Sharon, author. | Rooney, Ellen, illustrator.
Title: The heart of the storm : a biography of Sue Bird / Sharon Mentyka ;
illustrated by Ellen Rooney.
Description: Seattle : Little Bigfoot | Sasquatch Books, [2022] | Series:
Growing to Greatness | Audience: Ages 5-9 years | Audience: Grades K-1
Identifiers: LCCN 2021005753 | ISBN 9781632172884 (Hardcover)
Subjects: LCSH: Bird, Sue--Juvenile literature. | Women basketball
players--United States--Biography--Juvenile literature. | Seattle Storm
(Basketball team)--History--Juvenile literature. | Women's National
Basketball Association--Juvenile literature. | Basketball--United
States--History.
Classification: LCC GV884.B572 M46 2022 | DDC 796.323092 [B]--dc23
LC record available at https://lccn.loc.gov/2021005753

ISBN: 978-1-63217-288-4

Sasquatch Books
1904 Third Avenue, Suite 710
Seattle, WA 98101

SasquatchBooks.com